This book belongs to :

_____

Date :

Sermon :

Scripture :

Notes :

Take Away : This week I will focus on

Prayer Requests :

Upcoming Church Events & Opportunities :

Date :

Sermon :

Scripture :

Notes :

Take Away : This week I will focus on

Prayer Requests :

Upcoming Church Events & Opportunities :

Date:

Sermon:

Scripture:

Notes:

Take Away : This week I will focus on

Prayer Requests :

Upcoming Church Events & Opportunities :

Date :

Sermon :

Scripture :

Notes :

Take Away : This week I will focus on

Prayer Requests :

Upcoming Church Events & Opportunities :

Date :

Sermon :

Scripture :

Notes :

Take Away : This week I will focus on

Prayer Requests :

Upcoming Church Events & Opportunities :

Date :

Sermon :

Scripture :

Notes :

Take Away : This week I will focus on

Prayer Requests :

Upcoming Church Events & Opportunities :

Date :

Sermon :

Scripture :

Notes :

Take Away: This week I will focus on

Prayer Requests:

Upcoming Church Events & Opportunities:

Date :

Sermon :

Scripture :

Notes :

Take Away: This week I will focus on

Prayer Requests:

Upcoming Church Events & Opportunities:

Date :

Sermon :

Scripture :

Notes :

Take Away : This week I will focus on

Prayer Requests :

Upcoming Church Events & Opportunities :

Date :

Sermon :

Scripture :

Notes :

Take Away: This week I will focus on

Prayer Requests:

Upcoming Church Events & Opportunities:

Date :

Sermon :

Scripture :

Notes :

Take Away: This week I will focus on

Prayer Requests:

Upcoming Church Events & Opportunities:

Date :

Sermon :

Scripture :

Notes :

Take Away : This week I will focus on

Prayer Requests :

Upcoming Church Events & Opportunities :

Date :

Sermon :

Scripture :

Notes :

Take Away : This week I will focus on

Prayer Requests :

Upcoming Church Events & Opportunities :

Date :

Sermon :

Scripture :

Notes :

Take Away: This week I will focus on

Prayer Requests:

Upcoming Church Events & Opportunities:

Date :

Sermon :

Scripture :

Notes :

Take Away: This week I will focus on

Prayer Requests:

Upcoming Church Events & Opportunities:

Date :

Sermon :

Scripture :

Notes :

Take Away : This week I will focus on

Prayer Requests :

Upcoming Church Events & Opportunities :

Date :

Sermon :

Scripture :

Notes :

Take Away: This week I will focus on

Prayer Requests:

Upcoming Church Events & Opportunities:

Date :

Sermon :

Scripture :

Notes :

Take Away: This week I will focus on

Prayer Requests:

Upcoming Church Events & Opportunities:

Date :

Sermon :

Scripture :

Notes :

Take Away : This week I will focus on

Prayer Requests :

Upcoming Church Events & Opportunities :

Date :

Sermon :

Scripture :

Notes :

Take Away : This week I will focus on

Prayer Requests :

Upcoming Church Events & Opportunities :

Date :

Sermon :

Scripture :

Notes :

Take Away : This week I will focus on

Prayer Requests :

Upcoming Church Events & Opportunities :

Date :

Sermon :

Scripture :

Notes :

Take Away: This week I will focus on

Prayer Requests:

Upcoming Church Events & Opportunities:

Date :

Sermon :

Scripture :

Notes :

Take Away: This week I will focus on

Prayer Requests:

Upcoming Church Events & Opportunities:

Date :

Sermon :

Scripture :

Notes :

Take Away : This week I will focus on

Prayer Requests :

Upcoming Church Events & Opportunities :

Date :

Sermon :

Scripture :

Notes :

Take Away : This week I will focus on

Prayer Requests :

Upcoming Church Events & Opportunities :

Date :

Sermon :

Scripture :

Notes :

Take Away : This week I will focus on

Prayer Requests :

Upcoming Church Events & Opportunities :

Date :

Sermon :

Scripture :

Notes :

Take Away : This week I will focus on

Prayer Requests :

Upcoming Church Events & Opportunities :

Date :

Sermon :

Scripture :

Notes :

Take Away : This week I will focus on

Prayer Requests :

Upcoming Church Events & Opportunities :

Date :

Sermon :

Scripture :

Notes :

Take Away: This week I will focus on

Prayer Requests:

Upcoming Church Events & Opportunities:

Date :

Sermon :

Scripture :

Notes :

Take Away: This week I will focus on

Prayer Requests:

Upcoming Church Events & Opportunities:

Date :

Sermon :

Scripture :

Notes :

Take Away : This week I will focus on

Prayer Requests :

Upcoming Church Events & Opportunities :

Date :

Sermon :

Scripture :

Notes :

Take Away : This week I will focus on

Prayer Requests :

Upcoming Church Events & Opportunities :

Date :

Sermon :

Scripture :

Notes :

Take Away : This week I will focus on

Prayer Requests :

Upcoming Church Events & Opportunities :

Date :

Sermon :

Scripture :

Notes :

Take Away: This week I will focus on

Prayer Requests:

Upcoming Church Events & Opportunities:

Date :

Sermon :

Scripture :

Notes :

Take Away : This week I will focus on

Prayer Requests :

Upcoming Church Events & Opportunities :

Date:

Sermon:

Scripture:

Notes:

Take Away: This week I will focus on

Prayer Requests:

Upcoming Church Events & Opportunities:

Date :

Sermon :

Scripture :

Notes :

Take Away : This week I will focus on

Prayer Requests :

Upcoming Church Events & Opportunities :

Date:

Sermon:

Scripture:

Notes:

Take Away : This week I will focus on

Prayer Requests :

Upcoming Church Events & Opportunities :

Date :

Sermon :

Scripture :

Notes :

Take Away : This week I will focus on

Prayer Requests :

Upcoming Church Events & Opportunities :

Date :

Sermon :

Scripture :

Notes :

Take Away : This week I will focus on

Prayer Requests :

Upcoming Church Events & Opportunities :

Date :

Sermon :

Scripture :

Notes :

Take Away : This week I will focus on

Prayer Requests :

Upcoming Church Events & Opportunities :

Date :

Sermon :

Scripture :

Notes :

Take Away : This week I will focus on

Prayer Requests :

Upcoming Church Events & Opportunities :

Date :

Sermon :

Scripture :

Notes :

Take Away : This week I will focus on

Prayer Requests :

Upcoming Church Events & Opportunities :

Date :

Sermon :

Scripture :

Notes :

Take Away : This week I will focus on

Prayer Requests :

Upcoming Church Events & Opportunities :

Date :

Sermon :

Scripture :

Notes :

Take Away : This week I will focus on

Prayer Requests :

Upcoming Church Events & Opportunities :

Date :

Sermon :

Scripture :

Notes :

Take Away : This week I will focus on

Prayer Requests :

Upcoming Church Events & Opportunities :

Date :

Sermon :

Scripture :

Notes :

Take Away: This week I will focus on

Prayer Requests:

Upcoming Church Events & Opportunities:

Date :

Sermon :

Scripture :

Notes :

Take Away: This week I will focus on

Prayer Requests:

Upcoming Church Events & Opportunities:

Date :

Sermon :

Scripture :

Notes :

Take Away : This week I will focus on

Prayer Requests :

Upcoming Church Events & Opportunities :

Date :

Sermon :

Scripture :

Notes :

Take Away : This week I will focus on

Prayer Requests :

Upcoming Church Events & Opportunities :

Made in United States
North Haven, CT
23 November 2024